in**t**ercession

Cricket Aull, SFO

Intercession
Cricket Aull, SFO
Copyright © 2006, Cricket Aull, SFO

Cover Image: IstockPhoto.com
Cover and book design: Mary Farag - Tau publishing design department

For information regarding permission, write to:
Tau Publishing,
Attention: Permissions Dept.
1422 East Edgemont Avenue
Phoenix, AZ 85006

ISBN: 978-1-935257-48-6

First Edition, 2010
10 9 8 7 6 5 4 3 2 1

Published by Tau Publishing, Phoenix, AZ
For reorders and other inspirational materials visit out website.

Tau-publishing.com
Words and Works of Inspiration

Contents

A Living Prayer

It was said of St. Francis of Assisi,
that when he prayed he was not so much
praying as becoming himself a prayer.
May these words assist you in becoming a

living prayer.

*I*n years of giving spiritual direction, it has been my experience that many people who feel called to intercessory prayer, have little understanding of this gift and the depth to which one may be taken in prayer. They may sense a need for intercession or a drawing to it, but for the most part, remain unfamiliar with the extent to which God may use the individual in this calling. As faith-filled people of the Gospel of Christ, we are all called to prayer. Intercession is offered especially as prayer for others, and therefore, becomes more effective as we unite those intercessions to Christ, who is *"at the right hand of God, who indeed intercedes for us."* (Rom. 8:34) Intercession, then, is first about our relationship with the Lord, and allowing His intercessions to become a part of our lives. Some people are led into this more deeply than others. For those who are, I hope to bring some clarity and direction, so that we, as prayerful people, may better understand our union with God as we pray for others and for the world.

Lord,

I come before You as Your servant of intercessory prayer. I ask that Your faithful guidance illumine my understanding and deepen my faith, so that I may be able to pray in pure and effective ways for the needs of others.

Amen.

I

$\mathcal{P}$ reparing $\mathcal{O}$ ur $\mathcal{H}$ eart

$\mathcal{T}$ he dictionary has two meanings for the word 'intercession.' It can be 1) an entreaty in favor of another, or it can be 2) a mediation in a dispute.[1] Intercession is used in scripture to mean: prayer, making a petition, interceding in behalf of another, to entreat, to light upon, to meet together. [2]

In the Bible we see this word used in reference to approaching God, or a king, in order to be heard on behalf of others. The Old Testament gives us a good example of this in Moses. When the Lord was angered by the Israelites, seeing *"how stiff-necked this people is,"* it was Moses who implored the Lord saying, *"Why, O Lord, should your wrath blaze up against your own people ... with such great power and with so strong a hand?"* (Ex.32:9,11) Moses reminded the Lord of the promise he had made to Abraham and his descendants, so that in verse 14 we read that *"the Lord relented in the punishment he had threatened to inflict on his people."* It was also Moses who went before God when the Israelites sinned in building the golden calf. Moses entreated God saying, *"If you would only forgive their sin! If you will not, then strike me out of the book that you have written."* (Ex.32:32) We may find it somewhat remarkable that Moses is willing to accept this punishment when he was not guilty of their sin. But the prophet Isaiah mentions this same acceptance in one of the Suffering Servant chapters. Chapter 53 of Isaiah ends with the words describing the Savior, *"yet he bore the sin of many, and made intercession for the transgressors."* (Is. 53:12)

Romans 8:34 speaks of this as Christ's intercession, *"It is Christ Jesus, who died, yes, who was raised from the dead, who is at the right hand of God, who indeed intercedes for us."* Hebrews 7:25 adds even more to this consoling message: *"Consequently he is able for all time to save those who draw near to God through him, since he always lives to make intercession for them."* These scriptures reveal some very meaningful thoughts to us about intercession. First, they are reminding us that Jesus is praying for us in a very present way even now. How blessed we are, and how thankful we should be, for his intercession. Christ's loving care for our salvation and sanctification did not end with the crucifixion and resurrection. He *still* 'lives to make intercession' on our behalf. Also, we know that Jesus is praying for us in a most perfect way. We pray imperfectly, but he knows exactly what we need and prays always what is best. We should be praying everyday that *we can fulfill* the prayers he prays for us. Because he is interceding in a perfect way for us, we should want to be perfectly united to him in those prayers. I do not want to pray in any way that is different or contrary to his intercession. It is our 'union with Christ' that is especially important for us as intercessors and makes this gift of prayer more effective.

Our *capacity to love* is a very necessary part of intercession. Often without our awareness, God is deepening our hearts to have a greater ability to love. We may see this deepening in our hearts at times of feeling very blessed and loved, but it is present, on another level, in our painful trials, misunderstandings, and sorrow. God uses these difficult times especially to increase our capacity to love, and when this occurs, our hearts are more properly prepared to intercede for others. Persecution can purify our desire to seek the truth, at the same time it humbles us to live that truth in love. Painful rejection can make us sensitively careful to never reject others, so that we love in *all circumstances*, as does Christ. Trials of sorrow, doubt and confusion can bring us into God's presence with greater abandonment, where the Holy Spirit can work without hindrance. The more deeply we enter a life in Christ, the more emptied and fashioned we become as instruments for intercession. God is leading us to become Christ-like, and in this likeness, we can pray with Christ's heart.

I can look back over my own life and see many ways that God used my sorrow as a way of drawing me closer to himself. I can see that my personal pain gave me a genuine sensitivity toward others, and a greater desire to bring the comfort and healing of Christ to them. I have no doubt that those experiences of suffering provided the very transformation I needed to love more purely. Since it is love that heals, it is love that should be increased and perfected in the intercessor. So we embrace those sorrows that call us more perfectly into knowing God's love. It is important though, to turn all of our trials and sorrows to God *without resentment*, but with confident trust in his constant care for us. We trust always in his will, his goodness, and his love. We can be assured that even in our sufferings, *"all things work for good for those who love God, who are called according to his purpose."* (Rom. 8:28)

Our confident turning to God leads more and more to the correct docility of heart we need for intercessory prayer. We have received this 'gift of intercession' from the Lord, and we need to accept it with the simple desire to make ourselves available to the Lord's use. Is God able to move freely in our hearts, or does the Holy Spirit's guidance meet with resistance in us? Are we pliable, like the soft clay that can easily be molded in the potter's hands, or do we pray with half hardened hearts that only see things our way? Intercession can take us into a variety of needs and people. Docility of heart makes us more understanding of each one so that we can pray appropriately. Coupled with this docility is the need to develop inner stillness. Stillness brings our heart before the Lord saying, "I am putting all else aside, so that You have room to work and lead as You will." We must take the time to become still before the Lord and learn to wait upon the Holy Spirit's guidance. There are always areas of need in the people or situations we bring into prayer which we have no way of knowing. An inner stillness will make us sensitive to the Holy Spirit who sees those things that are hidden from our natural eyes, so that we can be led to pray with more clear and specific direction. As in all our prayers, it is the Spirit who *"helps us in our weakness; for we do not know how to pray as we ought ... "* (Rom. 8:26)

> **Lord, create in my heart this receptivity to the Holy Spirit's guidance. Help me to acquire inner stillness, docility of heart, and a greater capacity to bear Your love. These are all qualities I need for deeper prayer, but I cannot grow in these graces without Your help. I trust You to take me to this deeper place of loving and living for You. Amen.**

II

Developing a Prayerful Disposition

---

*P*rayer is most powerful when the prayer need is 'in God's hands,' so it is understandable that the intercessor needs to become the prayerful point of releasing this need to God. Intercession is more than simply the words or thoughts of prayer. Intercession is, in a sense, *becoming a part* of the prayer. For the intercessor, this involves two things. First, is an ever deepening union with God. We saw this union in Moses, in the extended time he spent in prayer. He sought God's presence, God's instruction, and even God's favor. For us, as well, this union with God means that we are turned to the Lord both outwardly and interiorly, always filtering our situation through God's guidance and example. There is a constant flow of giving and receiving – the back and forth exchange of God's love with our love, God's will becoming our will, and God's presence continually transforming our presence. In all things, at all times, our intercession consciously includes our Lord because it is he who adds life and depth and meaning to all we do.

Secondly, out of this union with God, the intercessor is also united in a special way to the intercessions that are made. This, too, we saw in Moses, as previously stated: the intercessor has a willingness to accept the intercession with a greater personal commitment. In praying to God for a person or situation, the intercessor becomes a kind of spiritual 'interceptor' for the trials and difficulties that are taking place. This interception is made in the sense that our intercession directs those trials to God, and then prayerfully exchanges them for God's presence, God's healing, and God's love. Like an emptied vessel open for giving and receiving, there is a necessary connection and spiritual exchange being made. The prayers of the intercessor assist in offering the need to God, and also assist in offering God's help to the need.

Such a constant and necessary communion with God would need to involve our whole being – heart, mind, words and actions; our interior disposition being just as important as our exterior response. Interiorly, this disposition would include God being foremost in our heart and foremost on our mind. Exteriorly, it would mean that everything we do attempts to be in imitation of Christ. For such a disposition to dwell in us, three particular areas should be in proper place: our flesh, our thoughts, and our desires. These areas are a part of every intercession we make, and therefore, should be correctly united to God in our prayers. More specifically, we are uniting those areas to God's love which is omnipresent, omniscient, and omnipotent. For intercession to be more effective, it needs to be lovingly focused and abandoned to: God's presence, God's knowledge, and God's power.

The Omnipresence of God and Our Physical Disposition

"I appeal to you therefore, brethren, by the mercies of God, to present your bodies as a living sacrifice, holy and acceptable to God, which is your spiritual worship." Rom. 12:1

God is present always and every where. Ps. 46:1 calls him, *"our refuge and strength, a very present help in trouble."* We, on the other hand, are very limited in our bodily presence, yet God uses our prayers and intercessions to reach people beyond our physical location. Paul urged Timothy to pray and make intercessions for kings and *"all who are in high positions."* (1 Tim.2:2) James 5:16 tells us to *"pray for one another, that you may be healed."* Prayer does not have to include our physical presence. If prayer is not limited by our particular location, what might limit, or even strengthen, it? The second part of James 5:16 reads, *"The fervent prayer of a righteous person is very powerful."* We could conclude from this scripture that there may be a correlation between the 'power' of the prayer and the 'righteousness' of the one praying it. We see this same correlation countless times in the lives of the saints. Their prayers were very effective because of their efforts to live in righteousness. Our intercession then, uses our physical body as instruments of prayer, but even more effectively when our body is offered to God in a 'holy and acceptable' way, as Romans 12:1 reads. Another scripture in Romans (6: 13) also speaks of this correlation: "present yourselves to God as raised from the dead to life and the parts of your bodies to God as weapons for (some translations read 'of') righteousness." For intercession to be more effective, our physical presence and 'disposition' need to embrace this 'striving for righteousness' which includes a proper detachment from self and the world. This allows our intercession to be made from a union with God's presence, rather than our own personal attachments. Our physical presence then, should embrace intercessory prayer with our own endeavors to grow toward holiness. With this, we include an offering to God of our physical activity. I will give three examples of doing this.

First is in simple, everyday duties or obligations we have. Whatever we are already doing in our routine of the day, can be brought before God as a prayer for the person of our intercessions. What we do, we do with the extra effort to not complain, worry, or become impatient, so that the physical 'doing' is offered with a greater purity of love. As Paul wrote to the Philippians, we "do all things without grumbling or questioning … " (Phil. 2:14) Then, as we unite the prayers to the action we are already doing, we find ourselves involved in a more meaningful way and we 'offer' more of ourselves in the prayer. An example of using this for intercession could be an experience I had years ago when I was making a window covering for a sliding-glass door to our house. I was trying to get ready for the cold weather that was coming by making a window shade using a thick upholstery fabric. I had sewn the fabric, hung it over the door, and then realized that I had sewn the top in the wrong place. I had to start all over and this required cutting out each individual stitch I had just sewn, an especially difficult job because of the fabric I had used. But shortly after I began this painstaking procedure, I received a phone call from a close friend. Her father was dying, and she was at the hospital, calling to ask me to pray for him. I suddenly had a more meaningful way to intercede, and a more meaningful way to fulfill my present task. For the next hour I sat on the floor, cutting away each thread of this large piece of material; and as I separated each stitch from the fabric, I prayed for his soul to be separated from each attachment to the world. I prayed for physical attachments to be cut away, emotional attachments, mental attachments, all areas of sin and anything that might be keeping him from receiving the Lord. I prayed for his family to be able to release him. And I prayed for the restoration of his soul to God. I prayed for things I normally would not have thought of, but in the physical task I was doing, I was able to intercede with my physical presence and activity as well.

Secondly, our intercession is deepened by *choosing a physical sacrifice*, such as in fasting. We are reminded of this in Mark 9:29, (and Matt. 17:20) when the disciples inquired about the healing of a boy. Jesus told them, *"This kind can only come out through prayer"* (and a variant reading adds) *"and through fasting."* We can make a sacrifice of our own choosing in order to add a personal 'offering' to the prayers. It is a deeper 'giving of ourselves.' If we are interceding for someone who has an addiction, we can choose to give up something we have great enjoyment in, and unite that sacrifice to the person of our intercession. We may be praying for people in a country where hunger and starvation is a problem, so we, as an intercessor, choose to eat much less ourselves, in order to be more wholly united to those people in our prayers. There are often very obvious ways of uniting oneself physically with the intercession that is being prayed. I was giving a retreat once in which a woman who attended was in a wheel chair. She was sharing with the group that she used to be very active in the church and now felt much less useful because of her condition. Such feelings can easily lead one to depression and what is truly a 'less useful disposition'. I told her she was not by any means less useful, but that she was now becoming useful in a different way. Her intercessions, which she obviously had more time for, now had a continual 'living sacrifice' to offer that added a deeper dimension to all her prayers. Sometimes we are not aware of the value a personal sacrifice can add to our intercession; and I cannot stress enough how much even a small sacrifice, when made in sincere love, will add. This is explained further in *Understanding Penance*.[3] Since Christ's prayers for us included a great sacrifice, it is fitting and effective when we do the same.

Thirdly, on more rare occasions, *God may initiate this* 'uniting and sacrificing' in His own way. The Holy Spirit may, for instance, bring upon the intercessor a very profound 'sharing' of the sorrow, despair, or physical pain of the one being prayed for. At times in intercession, people who are praying very intently for another person, or many people, may begin to experience some aspect of the same suffering as the people for whom the prayers are intended. This can come in a physical, mental, or emotional way, just as the person receiving the prayers has need of healing and help in a physical, mental, or emotional way. I can usually ask very prayerful people who are experiencing a new and unexplained sorrow, anger, or mental depression if they have been praying specifically for someone else with these problems, and their answer confirms it. Their experience of suffering is 'outside' of, or unrelated to, their own present physical, mental, or emotional state. But they have become 'internally aware' of someone else's difficulty and so, they need to offer that pain for the person, or people, who are living it. As Paul reminds us in 1 Cor. 12:26, *"If one part suffers, all the parts suffer with it; if one part is honored, all the parts share its joy."* A clear understanding of how we 'offer to God' all that we suffer and endure is necessary to keep from entering into that sharing the wrong way. It is also important that this type of 'profound sharing' be initiated and led by the Holy Spirit and should not be anticipated. One should not, in any way, be looking for this to happen. Furthermore, it is a level of sharing that may be best to bring under the guidance of a spiritual director. If the intercessor is led in this way of intercession, whatever is being 'shared supernaturally' needs to be offered to

God with firm faith and sincere surrender to his will, remembering always that it is a 'surrender to the Lord' and not a 'surrender to the suffering' that is made. From years of intercessory prayer in my own life, and seeing God move in profound ways through intercession, I am convinced that our heavenly Father does not allow anyone to be alone in a suffering need. Even when a person may not be physically present, someone, somewhere, is united to them through the prayers of intercession. As God desires, he may allow the intercessor to transcend the physical limitations between one's self and the person in need. The intercessor's own faith and abandon to God are very important here for two reasons: First, because some level of this faith and trust in God is also 'shared profoundly' with the person receiving the prayers; and secondly, to insure that the intercessor's 'presence' is obedient and surrendered to the move of God's presence. To put it in other words: As the intercessor shares in the struggles and needs of a person, that person also shares in the faith and hope of the intercessor.

I have found that this third example may be the most misunderstood area of intercessory prayer: that our own physical presence, discomfort, and even our suffering, may be used by God as a part of the intercession we make. Instead, we tend to see Christ as the one who has done the physical suffering and dying, but forget that he has given us an example to follow. Paul saw himself as a 'joint heir with Christ' in his suffering, *"(we are) … heirs of God and joint heirs with Christ, if only we suffer with him so that we may also be glorified with him."* Rom. 8:17. Peter's letter to the Christians in Asia Minor encourages them to be *"patient when you suffer."* He called it *"a grace before God"* when the suffering came *"for doing what is good. … For to this you have been called, because Christ also suffered for you, leaving you an example that you should follow in his footsteps."* 1 Peter 2:20-21. And why would it be beneficial, or even necessary, *for us* to intercede for others with a physical sacrifice of our own? In part it is because, in our humanity, we have all helped in bringing one another to sin. So now, in our humanity, we have become 'a living sacrifice' *with Christ*, in order to help bring one another to God's healing. *"For as Christ's sufferings overflow to us, so through Christ does our encouragement also overflow."* 2 Cor. 1:5

The intercessor matures in this call to intercession as one's physical disposition matures in its yielding to the Lord. Do we have mastery over our senses – or do they master us? If the Holy Spirit is prompting us to add some sacrifice to our prayers, deny our body a particular enjoyment, or get up in the middle of the night to pray, is our body yielded to those promptings? Or do Paul's words in Romans 7:18 apply to us? *"The willing is ready at hand, but doing the good is not."* Intercession becomes more effective as the intercessor's disposition is one of *striving for holiness, and yielded to the will of the Lord.*

Lord, I offer to You my physical presence to be used as You desire. Help me to become yielded to Your will and Your guidance in all situations. Make me sensitive to the unity You so want us to have with one another, so that I become a more willing and caring part of the lives you entrust to my prayers. Please give me a greater desire to become holy so that I can be pleasing to You, and my prayers of intercession can draw others to Your love
Amen.

The Omnipresence of God and Our Mental Disposition

"Have no anxiety about anything, but in everything by prayer and supplication with thanksgiving let your requests be made known to God. And the peace of God which passes all understanding, will keep your hearts and your minds in Christ Jesus." Phil.4:6-7

God is all-knowing, while we are always limited in knowledge. For intercession to be more effective in our thoughts, our mental 'disposition' needs to be steadfast in faith and focused upon God. At times, when we pray for a need or something we want very much to happen, we can be praying *to* God, but the deeper and more constant place of our thoughts are only on that need we have in prayer. We are thinking how great the need is, wondering how it can be turned around, or how we might be able to accomplish a solution. It is God we are directing the need to, and God we should be thinking of with confidence and gratitude. Our thoughts should be upon 'seeing' that the need is in God's hands. Another way to realize where our mind is really focused is by examining our hope. Sometimes we find in prayer that our hope is not in God at all, but only in whether or not we will receive what we have prayed for. If our hope is truly *in God*, and not the end result, we are never disappointed. Examine the real focus of your thoughts. Examine your level of hope and purity of faith when you are in prayer. We come into prayer for such and such a thing to happen. Are we doing that with the singular focus of directing that need toward God? Or, do we pray for that need and at the same time constantly worry about the outcome? Pure faith reminds us to pray constantly, but with surrender to God, and with thanksgiving that shows we have correctly surrendered the need to him. Continuing to dwell on the negative brings a lack of faith into our intercession. *"Instead, seek his kingdom, and these things shall be yours as well."* Lk12:31 The focus of our faith needs to be 'concrete' in a sense, more real to us than that worry or sorrow we may have over the situation. When our faith is *purely in God*, it is in the position of 'moving mountains' that Jesus speaks of in Matt. 17:20.

We should be trying, at all times, to develop in prayer an interior disposition in which God fills and sustains our thoughts. In our prayers, God is foremost. We can be aware of the need, or the person for whom we pray, but all the while, our inner vision is set upon how great God is, how loving God is, or how perfect God is, and so forth. Nothing in the need of our prayers becomes larger or more consuming than our focus on God who is always perfect, loving, and good. Intercession is meant to carry, strengthen, and hold the natural need before God's supernatural grace, so the intercessor's mind needs to be confidently turned to God's goodness. As it is with our 'presence' in prayer, the deepest intercession is led by the Holy Spirit, who will lead us into areas of prayer that go beyond our human understanding. So we, at times, have to be taken beyond our human understanding to a deeper union with God's knowledge. The necessary disposition of the intercessor's mind is that of being *emptied* of *self-focus* and *centered on God with confident faith*. We offer all of our thoughts for God to work in place of our own understanding. Proverbs 3:5-6 tells us, *"do not rely on your own insight. In all your ways acknowledge him, and he will make straight your paths."*

I remember an experience once of coming into a deep realization of God's omniscience. I had been praying very much for a particular need that involved certain people in my life, and at one point, while I was praying in church, I suddenly had a very vivid memory of a time that God revealed something to me when I was 12 years old. I was seeing that whole event as though it was right before me again. But now I saw - with the clearest understanding - that at that time when I was 12, God had *complete knowledge* of everything I would be praying for *now* – 40 years later. He had spoken to me then, knowing exactly what people would be in my life at this present time. He knew where I would be living and all that I would need. It was so clear to me that God saw *all things*, even before they came into being, I could only think to myself, "How easy it should be to surrender our lives to an All-Knowing God. Why do we *ever doubt* our Lord who knows all things with such perfect knowledge, and holds all knowledge in such perfect love?"

Lord, I give You my thoughts and all my understanding. May I always remember that You hold all knowledge and wisdom within Yourself, and I need to come to You continuously for what I, myself, need to know. Help me to release the rest into Your hands and remain peacefully focused on Your goodness, Your love, and Your perfect, omniscient authority. Amen.

The Omnipresence of God and Our Heart's Disposition

" ... You shall love the Lord your God with all your heart, and with all your soul, and with all your mind, and with all your strength. The second is this: "You shall love your neighbor as yourself." Mark 12:30-31

God is all-powerful, while we have only the power God gives us by means of our free will. But what a great power that becomes for us! It is clear that we are not more powerful than God, yet if we choose to love and serve God, his power works on our behalf. Likewise, of ourselves - and without God, we possess no power that is greater than evil. Yet if choosing evil becomes the desire of our heart, such a power will have access into our lives. We often fail to see how much 'power' we possess in our simple choices of free will. For intercession to be more effective and powerful, our heart needs to be in proper place with God, always wanting to come to God with *pure desire for him*. We should be seeking God more than anything else for which we are praying. The Psalmist writes, *"My soul thirsts for thee like a parched land."* (Ps. 143:6) Such a 'thirsting' should be at the heart of all our desires. It is the Lord we are attending to first in our prayers. This is the kind of purity that needs to be in our intercession, *"Not my will but Thine be done."* The intercession we are called to enter can best be carried out with the disposition described in the scripture above from Mark 12. *"You shall love the Lord your God with all your heart, and with all your soul, and with all your mind, and with all your strength."* This was the answer Christ gave to the scribe who asked which commandment was the greatest. A pure desire for God will give us a pure desire for interceding and loving others, so that we fulfill the second part, *"You shall love your neighbor as yourself."* But this love involves our whole self as the scripture reads: heart, soul, mind and strength. So, it is not effective or truthful to offer our heart to God, but not our thoughts, or to offer our thoughts, and practice a rejection of God's will in our bodies. Intercession involves our whole self – loving, serving, and living for God. It is in 'living for God' that we find ourselves best equipped to live for others and serve them with the gift of intercession.

Our prayers are one of the ways God reaches people with His love, so it is understandable that in offering these prayers, our own heart should be filled with the love that we *are praying forth* for others to receive. Our fears should be released. Anxiousness, sorrow and resentments cannot be held within us. We should be careful, in our intercessions, to not 'take upon ourselves' the heaviness of someone else's doubt or fear, in a way that causes us to lose faith or love. We have to be able to release it to the Lord. The intercessor is only the instrument of prayer that offers the need up to God, and then prays with - and for - faith and love of God in return. Our disposition of heart then, is to *love God first - and wholly*. This will be accompanied by a *pure desire to love* that serves his will in place of our own. In this way, we are able to be led with a more correct sense of 'how to pray' and also 'how long to pray.' We become more and more receptive to God's leading so that we can 'pray it through' to completion. Sometimes we may be interceding for only a few minutes or a few hours. At other times an intercession can continue for a few months or even years. We learn how to 'keep vigil' with our prayers, and we develop an inner awareness or sensitivity to when 'it is finished,' and we do not stop until it is. Our call to prayer is in God's timing, not our own.

The intercession we are called to may not be about a particular person or need that is obvious. It may be something completely unknown to us. Several years ago, I felt strongly led to stay after Mass each day and pray for people to enter into a time of stillness before God. Everyday I would go to Mass, and every day I could not leave at the end because of the strong desire inside of me to pray for stillness to enter people's hearts. I often would stay an hour after everyone else had left the church and pray only for that one thing. I remember getting discouraged after weeks of this because I did not have a more specific purpose for my intercession, and I wondered if my prayers were making any difference. A few months went by and I was speaking with my spiritual director who made the comment to me, "Never underestimate the power of your prayers." It was a small, but needed word of encouragement. And that evening, I was able to see how true it was. I was attending a seminar at our church. At one point in the evening everyone was divided into small groups and told to pray that God would reveal to each of us a word we needed to receive from him. After about 20 minutes of silent prayer in our group, one of the men suddenly said, "I need to be spending more time being still before the Lord. That is what he is saying to me." Almost immediately, another man said, "That is exactly what I am hearing, too. I don't spend enough time being still in God's presence so that he can speak to me." You can see from this example something else we should understand about intercession, and that is that some aspect of these prayers are for the intercessor as well. The intercession we pray will be doing something for us, in addition to those who are being lifted up to God in our intentions. It may be for our own encouragement, our own increased sensitivity, or a spiritual awareness we need. In this instance, I needed to learn that my prayers were truly being answered whether or not I understood the whole purpose behind them.

As intercessors we may feel, at times, like 'the voice of one crying in the wilderness.' In a sense, we are the voice of intercession in the wilderness of people's pain, and we are praying to 'make straight the way of the Lord.' When we have properly sought God and surrendered to him our flesh, our thoughts, and our desires, it 'clears the way' for the Lord's will, and makes the intercessor's prayers an effective instrument in God's hands. We must be able to take the presence, the knowledge, and the power 'out of our hands' and let those needs of intercession be answered by the omnipresence, omniscience, and omnipotence of God.

Lord, my heart is Yours. Please help me in those areas where I tend to desire something besides Your pure love and perfect will. Your power is perfectly united to Your plan for us. Let me trust in what You are doing and let me desire You above all things, so that I may love You purely and intercede for others with the purity that allows Your omnipotence to come forth. Amen.

III

The Importance of Purity

---

*P*urity is an important element of intercessory prayer because God, himself, brings this quality into our prayerful communion. When we come before God in prayer we should see that we are, in fact, in the presence of Divine Purity. We should desire, and pray for, the grace to be growing in purity ourselves so as to offer to God this reflection of himself. We begin to do this especially when our prayers are made with the pure desire of serving, in agreement with Christ's words, *"I am among you as one who serves."* Luke 22:27. This posture brings us to a deeper participation in prayer because it imitates the humble devotion that is in Christ.

Recalling what was written in our opening paragraph on page 1, we saw that one of the scriptural meanings for the word 'intercession' was 'to meet together.' That is what occurs in effective prayer. It is a true 'meeting' or a coming together of *purity from God* with a form of *purity from us*. This pure union creates the 'spiritual ground' where intercession is most fruitful.

Purity of Attention 1

Let us consider three ways that Divine Purity is present to us when we come into prayer. First, God gives us his pure *attention* when we pray. He is so attentive to us, it is as though no one else exists in the whole world. Just as he *loves each of us as if we were the only one he loved,* he is likewise able to be *attentive* to us as though we were the *only one praying* to him. So when we are in prayer, we are receiving from him, that which is the same as, 'his undivided attention.'

In return for God's gift of pure attention to us, we should bring into prayer our own pure and undivided *attention* toward God. Our mind needs to be set upon our Lord. We should not let distractions take our thoughts away from the holy presence of God we have been privileged to enter. For many though, staying focused while praying is difficult. The mind wanders easily and then discouragement takes over instead of effective prayer. For those times, I have found it helpful to remember how very present God is before me. I do this in two ways: First, I picture God being right in front of me when I pray. Psalm 100:2 tells us to *"Come into his presence with singing."* When I first read that Psalm in a Russian Bible years ago, I was quite surprised to notice that the words written in Russian literally meant, "Come before his face." That image has helped me to imagine a much closer 'presence' of God before me. He is close enough to hear a whisper, and he receives all the 'whispers of our heart' with greatest loving attention.

Secondly, because I have made myself aware of the Lord's face right before me, knowing also that he is *giving me* his pure and undivided attention, I pray so that the words have real meaning to me. If my mind has wondered, I stop and think about the words. And I repeat them so that they are coming from my heart. I even picture the prayer doing exactly what it says, so that I see it happening in my mind. In this way, I keep myself consciously involved in the prayers, and I remain focused on the Lord with constant *attention*.

Purity of Intention 2

In addition to pure attention, when we are in prayer God offers to us his pure *intention* for all areas of our life. He only wants and wills what is best for us. Whatever we are praying for, whatever we need, God will always want what is for our good. He does not want or will anything for us that is wrong, unkind, or unholy. There is purity in everything our Lord desires for our lives.

This too, is a purity we should return to God in prayer. We need to have pure *intentions* in our own heart. *"I am among you as one who serves"* should be our desire, as it is God's. We come into prayer wanting God's will to be done, as His will is always pure and best for us. For myself, I bring my intentions to God in this way: When I am praying, as I said, I also 'see' or imagine in my mind the prayer doing what the words say. If I am praying for God to help someone, I picture God doing this. If I am praying for myself to grow in patience or peace, I picture myself this way. I view this 'picture' as an act of my faith. I have not seen it in the natural, but I see it first with the eyes of faith. But then, as an act of surrender, I offer it to God to answer as He wills. I remove any 'hold' or clinging to it that I may have. I know that the Lord will always answer the prayer by doing what is best with my offering. And then, because I have set myself aside to serve His will instead of my own, there is a pure *intention* being offered. I desire only to have 'a servant's heart,' uniting myself completely to God's intention.

Purity in Everything Done 3

Thirdly, when we pray, there is complete purity in *all that God does*. The same purity God desires for us individually, he desires for everyone else at the same time. So, the *collection* of all other people we encounter is part of, and included in, the purity that the Lord is offering to us. What is best for us is also working in harmony with what is best for the people and situations around us. We can be assured there is purity in everything God is doing, whether it involves us directly or indirectly. What he wills for all of us is pure, and therefore, works *all things together for good*. Again, this is a purity we should be bringing before God in our prayers. How do we offer this purity to God in return?

It is by realizing that when we come to God in prayer we are also bringing with us *all that we have done* throughout the day. In prayer we bring before God the *collection* of everything we have thought or said or acted upon. What we are doing *outside of* our specific prayer time, is part of what we bring as an offering to God *in* our specific times of prayer. In other words, we need to be consistent with our words, our actions, and our prayers before God. Do we pray for something we need and then negate those prayers by speaking to everyone as though God will not help us? Do we ask for his guidance and then act in a way contrary to what we know is God's guidance – his will – in other areas? Do we pray with worry and complaining instead of faith and a steady focus on his goodness? We should be striving to live in purity our whole day, so that when we come before God in a time specifically of prayerful union with him, we bring a whole 'collection' of thoughts and words and actions that we have endeavored to make pure.

When the purity God offers to us is received with the purity of our own attention, intentions, and all we are doing, that is when prayer becomes especially powerful and unhindered. There is a great release of obstacles from prayers that are made - and united - in purity. In addition to this, all prayer should be balanced with *thankful anticipation* for the good that is always in God's heart and the *humility* that inspires a *sincere desire to serve* his will.

> *Dearest Lord, help me to desire purity in my attention, my intentions, and in all I do throughout the day. Allow me to pray with the pure and humble desire of being a servant in Your hands. I pray that my intercession would reflect Your own holy goodness that is void of self-glorification and longs to see others blessed and healed. Thank you for all the graces that assist me in my intercessions. Amen.*

IV

Spiritual Aids in Intercession

"For though we live in the world we are not carrying on a worldly war, for the weapons of our warfare are not worldly but have divine power to destroy strongholds. We destroy arguments and every proud obstacle to the knowledge of God, and take every thought captive to obey Christ, being ready to punish every disobedience, when your obedience is complete." 2 Cor. 10:3-6

We are given an abundance of spiritual aids to assist us in our intercessions: the power of many different prayer forms, along with praises to God and fasting, among others. Intercessory prayer can often be given more direction and strength through our use of these. I will only mention a few and only go into detail on some that are less understood. This scripture in 2nd Corinthians calls to our attention that the 'battles' we face are 'not worldly' but of a spiritual nature and therefore need to be handled with spiritual weapons. In intercessory prayer though, our intercession may not always appear to have this dimension of 'warfare' to which Paul refers. Whether it appears to or not, these spiritual aids will still be valuable for our sanctity and helpful to our prayer life. For those times in which a 'battle' would clearly describe the prayer we are in, we should always remember that: - we are never left or forsaken by God, - there is more going on that remains unseen to us so there is reason to remain steadfast, prayerful, and hopeful. And third, - God is always working for good, while the enemy is working toward destruction, but we choose who receives our attention.

Prayer

Our **prayers**, of course, are a primary weapon, whether they are spontaneous or written, whether they are from Holy Scripture, novenas, the rosary or other forms. Prayer is the basis of our intercession. We bring the need before God and we do so with prayers that we have been taught, or prayers that come from God's Word in scripture, prayers that we find meaningful from spiritual writings, or prayers that are inspired within us by the Holy Spirit. At times the prayer comes from such a depth it has no words. It is only held in our heart and offered with our whole being. Scripture tells us that there are times to pray in secret, (Matt 6:6), and times to pray in a multitude. (Luke 1:10) We are reminded in 1 Thess. 5:17 to *"pray constantly,"* in Luke 18:1 to *"pray and not lose heart"* and in 1 Timothy 2:8 to *"pray ... without anger or quarreling."* Paul also asks in his letter to Timothy that *"supplications, prayers, intercessions, and thanksgivings be made for all men, for kings and all who are in high positions, that we may lead a quiet and peaceable life, godly and respectful in every way."* 1 Tim.2:1-2

Prayers do not have to be long and drawn out. I have repeatedly seen situations turn around by God's grace after simply, but consistently, lifting up a particular need at regular intervals throughout the day, and ending the prayer with the Our Father, Hail Mary, and Glory Be.

I have found this simple way of praying for a need to be so special and effective, that I have made it a practice to stop and pray this way before certain routines of the day, like eating a meal or leaving the house. The prayer is short but focused, and then completely left in God's hands.

Fasting

In scripture, prayer is often combined with **fasting** when the need is more serious. Nehemiah fasted and prayed to God for mercy and help for the people of Israel. (Neh. 1:4) A fast was proclaimed in Ezra 8:21 to humble the people before God and make petitions for a safe journey. Esther asked that all the Jews in Susa hold a fast on her behalf before she approached the king to save her people. (Esther 4:16) Jesus fasted for forty days and nights in the wilderness before he began his public ministry. (Matt. 4:2)

Fasting is commonly thought of in connection to abstaining from food. The fasts typically mentioned in scripture were in this form. The idea of denying ourselves of something that is, at the same time, a necessity for living has many ways of helping our perspective and spiritual priorities. Fasting can aid us in simplifying our life in more ways than eating. Among other benefits, fasting causes us to acknowledge our need for God while it allows us to see and appreciate God's goodness and ability to sustain our lives. It makes real to us our limitations and our fleshly attachments. It prompts us, interiorly, to seek and depend on God rather than our selves. It helps to curb our desires for the world and break unholy attachments. It calls us to a more sincere commitment in whatever reason we are fasting. Fasting on a regular basis develops a more correct detachment between ourselves and those things we enjoy or dwell on, and this frees us from those subconscious tendencies we have of attending always to the needs of our flesh. It is precisely because food is a necessity for us, that its abstinence from time to time helps us gain a proper detachment toward all our earthly pleasures. The whole practice of *needing* what we cannot become *attached to* is beneficial to the soul, and moves us closer to God who fulfills both our needs and desires in himself. There is a caution, however, that should be understood here, in that fasting may sometimes lead to an attitude of spiritual pride. The spiritual benefit is not gained then, because the practice of fasting has resulted primarily in 'feeding' the ego. This leads us to examine the more pure signs of a fast, which we learn from the prophet Isaiah.

Although scripture usually mentions fasting in terms of abstaining from food, Isaiah, chapter 58 gives more meaning to this term:

> *"Is not this the fast that I choose: to loose the bonds of wickedness, to undo the thongs of the yoke, to let the oppressed go free, and to break every yoke? Is it not to share your bread with the hungry, and bring the homeless poor into your house; when you see the naked, to cover him, and not to hide yourself from your own flesh?" (Is. 58:6-7)*

Just previous to this, in verses 3-5, we are warned to not use fasting to *"seek your own pleasure."* Instead, it should be a fast that brings *"a day acceptable to the Lord."* Fasting can be abstaining from many things, in addition to food: habits we have, words we speak, actions we choose, or attitudes we hold.

We can fast by spending a day in silence from 'words' or in spending a week abstaining from 'unholy habits.' We can and should examine all things in our lives that need to be denied in order to make us *"holy and acceptable to God."* Isaiah 58 is telling us to make sure our fasting has a holy purpose and furthers in us an imitation of God's 'other-focused' nature, his loving care and concern for others. Adding an appropriate fast to our prayers of intercession would be another way of 'adding a sacrifice' (as mentioned earlier) to our prayers, and would still be in union with God's desire in Isaiah 58. It is a spiritual weapon we should not overlook.

Faith and Praise

Other 'weapons' that are powerful in prayer are also listed in scripture. In Matthew 17: 19-20 we see the necessity of sufficient **faith**. When the disciples asked Jesus why they could not cure the boy they were told, *"Because of your little faith."* Jesus said their faith had to be only as a grain of mustard seed to move a mountain, and *"nothing will be impossible to you."* In other places of the New Testament, there is healing of the paralytic, *"when Jesus saw their faith."* (Mark 2:5) We should note here, that it was the faith of the friends that Jesus was referring to in mentioning *their faith*. Scripture does not tell us what faith the paralytic himself had. In Matt. 9:29, sight is restored to two blind men with Jesus saying, *"According to your faith be it done to you."* Throughout scripture there is a connection between God's response and the person who has faith. Also, there is the exhortation we read in Ephesians 6:16, that tells us, *"above all"* to be using *"the shield of faith with which you can quench all the flaming darts of the evil one."*

Along with faith, the Old and New Testament also give accounts of God's moving among His people when glory and **praises to God** are sung. 2nd Chronicles, chapter 20 gives the account of *"a great multitude"* coming against Judah and all the inhabitants of Jerusalem. The people were told to not be afraid because the Lord would bring victory to them. And when those who were appointed *"began to sing and praise, the Lord set an ambush"* against those *"who had come against Judah, so that they were routed."* Another account of singing praises to God occurs in the New Testament, Acts 16:25-26, when Paul and Silas were in prison. As they were *"praying and singing hymns to God,"* there was a great earthquake and *"immediately all the doors were opened and everyone's fetters* were unfastened." I have had numerous times in my own life, too lengthy to explain here, in which praise and thanksgiving to God brought healing and help in unexpected and even miraculous ways. When Paul wrote to the Thessalonians to *"give thanks in all circumstances"* (5:18), he was not only writing this because of the praises that are due to God. He was reminding us that it is also beneficial *for us* when we give praise and thanksgiving to our Lord. The Psalmist knew this as well when writing Psalm 107:1-2, *"Give thanks to the Lord who is good, whose love endures forever! Let that be the prayer of the Lord's redeemed .... "* And Psalm 147:1, *"Praise the Lord! For it is good to sing praises to our God."*

Unity, God's Word, and Spiritual Armor

Something else that is mentioned in scripture, though often overlooked as a spiritual weapon, is **unity**. Paul writes of unity in his letter to the Philippians (1:27-28a), *"Only let your manner of life be worthy of the gospel of Christ, so that whether I come and see you or am absent, I may hear of you that you stand firm in one spirit, with one mind striving side by side for the faith of the gospel, and not frightened in anything by your opponents."* Chapter 2 of Philippians, verses 2 - 4, go on, *" ... complete my joy by being of the same mind, having the same love, being in full accord and of one mind. Do nothing from selfishness or conceit, but in humility count others better than yourselves. Let each of you look not only to his own interests, but also to the interests of others."* Paul's letter to the Ephesians also calls us to the importance of unity. He begins chapter 4 with the strong words: *"I ... beg you to lead a life worthy of the calling to which you have been called, with all lowliness and meekness, with patience, forbearing one another in love, eager to maintain the unity of the Spirit in the bond of peace. There is one body and one Spirit, just as you were called to the one hope that belongs to your call, one Lord, one faith, one baptism, one God and Father of us all, who is above all and through all and in all."* (Eph.

4:1-6) The third chapter of Colossians, verse 15, speaks of this unity: *"And let the peace of Christ rule in your hearts, to which indeed you were called in the one body."* The Psalmist, too, sings about unity, reminding us, *"How good it is, how pleasant, where the people dwell as one!"* concluding the psalm with the words, *"There the Lord has lavished blessing, life for evermore!"* (Ps. 133:1&3) And in John's gospel we see Jesus speaking about unity in His prayers for the Church, *"that they may all be one; even as thou, Father, art in me, and I in thee, that they also may be in us, so that the world may believe that thou hast sent me."* (John 17:21)

We sometimes fail to acknowledge the importance of unity, even between the Father, the Son, and the Holy Spirit. Do we consider what power would be present in the Holy Trinity if not for this perfect unity? Furthermore, how faithfully do we keep *ourselves* in union with God, realizing that *"the branch cannot bear fruit by itself, unless it abides in the vine … "*? (John 15:4) And how deeply can God be united to us, if we are not willing to become united to each other? Unity should be given particular attention in intercessory prayer because of the intercessor's special connection to the people that need to be 'held in prayer' before God. We might consider our prayers as a way of 'grafting others to the vine' that is Christ. In my observation, people seldom make unity a priority in their lives, or think of it as vitally important like the air we breathe or the food we need. Yet, in the kingdom of God, that is how valuable unity is. The whole heavenly host dwells in complete and perfect unity, and it greatly benefits us in our prayers when we strive to live this as Christ has asked. We can only live it, though, in the way Paul has described in the above quoted letters, *"with all lowliness and meekness, with patience, forbearing one another in love … "* and as we *"do nothing from selfishness or conceit, but in humility count others better than yourselves."* (Eph 4:2, Phil. 2:3)

Using **Holy Scripture** in the words of our prayers can be especially helpful as a form of intercession. Deuteronomy 8:3 tells us that *"man does not live by bread alone, but that man lives by everything that proceeds out of the mouth of the Lord."* I continually discover that people are not accustomed to using scripture as a way of interceding, yet the Word of God is *"living and active, sharper than any two-edged sword, piercing to the division of soul and spirit ... "* (Heb. 4:12) We use scripture as a form of prayer in the Liturgy of the Hours and throughout the Mass. Psalm 51:10 (or 12), for instance, calls us to pray: *"Create in me a clean heart, O God, and put a new and right spirit within me."* We pray the words of scripture in our Responsorial Psalms, such as Psalm 33:22, *"Lord, let your mercy be on us, as we place our trust in you."* We should be careful, however, to pray these words as *"living and active,"* believing that when we say them, they are taking place and coming to life within us. I often use scripture as a prayer for particular situations when God's word applies appropriately to that need. And I have seen God answer prayers in amazing ways just from praying scripture everyday for a person or situation. This should not be surprising though, since we are reminded in Isaiah that God's word *"shall not return to* (God) *empty,"* and, the prophet Jeremiah reminds us that God is *"watching over* (His) *word to perform it."* (Is. 55:11, Jer. 1:12) I have often encouraged others to pray the words of Col. 1:9-14 for their loved ones who need to grow in spiritual wisdom and understanding, 2 Thess. 1:11-12 for those who need to be strengthened in their vocation, Psalms 27 or 91 for knowing the comfort of God's safety, or 2 Cor. 9:8-12 for greater faith in God's provision. A scripture that I have prayed for years is taken from the words in Isaiah 50:4. I have prayed it as a prayer for myself and it has, no doubt, helped me in intercessory prayer: "Lord, please give me *'the tongue of those who are taught, that I may know how to sustain with a word him that is weary.'"* Praying in the form of Holy Scripture 'covers' our intercession with words that draw us to God's truth and increase our faith.

God's word is mentioned also in Paul's letter to the Ephesians as being a part of our **spiritual armor**. Chapter 6 describes this armor, with verse 17 reminding us to *"take the helmet of salvation, and the sword of the Spirit, which is the word of God."* Verse 13 tells us to take on the *"whole armor of God, that you may be able to withstand in the evil day, and having done all, to stand."* There is a 'spiritual readiness' that we have when this *armor* becomes a deeper part of our being. It includes *truth*, our *righteousness*, the *gospel of peace*, our *faith*, our *salvation*, and the *word of God*. Sometimes the weapon that is needed most is simply the **perseverance** we see at the end of verse 13. I hear from many people who get discouraged in their call to prayer. They have 'done all to stand' as this scripture describes, but still feel defeated in their prayers because they have seen nothing happen. In some cases our answer to prayer has only been delayed because our time of waiting is meant to help us grow in faith or patient endurance. Perseverance is often a part of intercession. When we have done all that is needed, we then need to remember this sometimes 'culminating point of intercession' that is simply to stand our ground and wait in faith.

The word 'to stand' that is used in this scripture from Ephesians is 'histemi' in Greek. It is perhaps an interesting coincidence that this word has the same beginning as the word 'historeo' in Greek, which means 'to be knowing or learned.'[4] Perhaps we can learn from these two words that when we have truly 'learned' our place of faith in God, it brings us to the point of 'standing firm.' James 4:7 offers this encouragement about a firm standing: *"Resist the devil and he will flee from you."* Very often we have not resisted to the point that *nothing* will deter, distract, or discourage us. Yet that is the point of 'standing firm' we need to reach in our intercessions. *"I wait for the Lord, my soul waits, and in his word I hope."* (Psalm 130:5)

Practicing Virtue

We read in the lives of the saints about other 'spiritual weapons.' Catherine of Siena drove the devil away by her **humility**. His words about her were recorded this way: "Damnable woman! There is no getting at you! If I throw you down in confusion you lift yourself up to mercy. If I exalt you, you throw yourself down. You come even to hell in your humility, and even in hell you hound me. So I will not come back to you again, because you beat me with the cudgel of charity!" [5]

St. Francis of Assisi, we are told by St. Bonaventure, "was armed with supernatural weapons and the more violently they (the devil and his demons) attacked him, the more courageous he was in **practicing virtue** and the more fervent in prayer. Then he would say with all confidence to the demons, "Do what you can to me, wicked and deceitful spirits. You can do nothing beyond what God allows you and I will be more than happy to suffer everything that God has decided I should endure." The devils in their pride could not stand such **steadfast courage**, and they retreated in confusion."[6] In another writing, the Mirror of Perfection, it is written that St. Francis used to say, "the devils are delighted when they discover means to quench or disturb the devotion and joy which springs from true prayer and other **holy practices** … Therefore … since this **spiritual joy** springs from **cleanness of heart** and the **purity of constant prayer**, it must be your first concern to acquire and preserve these two virtues, so as to possess this inward joy."[7]

It is clear in reading the lives of the saints that they won their battles and conflicts through ways of holiness rather than ways of the world. While we may not be battling the presence of evil in the way some of the saints did, our conflicts still require us to take all of our thoughts *"captive to obey Christ"* and to keep ourselves faithful to loving and serving God with pure hearts. We are *"in the world"* but we are meant to *"destroy arguments and every proud obstacle"* by living the way Christ has shown us in the Gospel. (2 Cor.10:3-6)

One of the virtues we find in the gospel is Christ's **obedience**. Scripture tells us that Christ *"became obedient unto death."* (Phil.2:8) Christ does *"only what he sees the Father doing."* (Jn 5:19) He does nothing on his own authority but speaks *"as the Father taught"* him. (Jn 8:28) Christ's 'food' was even *"to do the will of him who sent me, and to accomplish his work."* (Jn 4:34) *"For this reason the Father loves me, because I lay down my life … "* (Jn 10:17) Obedient doing, obedient speaking, obedient dying; all signs of the complete obedience Christ shows for the Father.

In the scripture from 2 Cor. 10:6, Paul is putting an emphasis on *our* complete obedience. It is worthwhile to take a closer look at these words. The word 'obedience' that is used here is 'hupakoe' in Greek. It means 'compliance' or 'submission' and comes from a similar word that means 'to conform to a command' or 'listen attentively.' Paul writes of this compliance as being 'complete' meaning: 'fulfilled, accomplished, or finished.' Such obedience would be constantly faithful. Furthermore, we are told in this scripture that when our obedience is complete, we are ready to 'revenge, vindicate, or retaliate' every disobedience.[8] What does this mean for us? It means that those who are living in obedience and faithfulness to God will be 'fulfilling or accomplishing' a faithful reflection of Christ which will open the doors of grace to reveal the truth; and in the light of that truth, disobedience can be seen for what it is, and obedience to God can be sought in its place. There are many examples of this, but one that is well known is the story of Shadrach, Meshach, and Abednego who were cast into the fiery furnace for their obedience in serving God rather that King Nebuchadnezzar. (Daniel 3) God used their obedience to reveal the truth of His power, and in that light of truth, King Nebuchadnezzar was able to perceive God and he was changed.

It is important to note, however, that obedience can lose value as a spiritual aid when the motive for this response is only obligation and the act is void of love. Christ's example of obedience is always an *act of love* for the Father. In addition to our own 'acts of love' for God, our intercession can be helped by the spiritual aids that are available to us in fasting, faith, praise, spiritual armor, God's word, the sacraments, and in practicing virtue.

> *Lord, I trust in Your constant care for my well-being. I trust in Your promise to never leave me or forsake me. When I am feeling discouraged or distracted, let me remember that You give me abundant resources in spiritual help. Let me not grow weary in praying for others. May I especially desire to grow in virtue and spiritual joy, so that You are glorified in all I do. Amen.*

V

Five Helpful Points of Intercession

On a few occasions I have heard the comment, "I will pray for these people, but I cannot change their free will." Two things need to be clarified about such a view. First, it sounds somewhat as though a defeat is already expected, which is not the mustard seed of 'pure faith' we are to take into prayer. But secondly, we do not need to change a person's free will in order for prayer to be effective. Rather, our prayers help the person *freely choose* what is good.

Consider those for whom you are praying in this way: Each person God created has been given a soul, and placed within that soul is the gift of free will. Original sin has already had an affect on this, as well as the influence of continuing sin around us. That affect of sin we will picture as being a large net that covers the soul. This net is somewhat loose, so the soul is not restricted from moving in its free will. It is simply 'encumbered' and looks more burdened than bound. However, every time the individual chooses to sin, another piece of this netting is added or secured. If the soul continues to reject God's grace for conversion, it finds itself in such a great covering of this restricting net, it becomes increasingly more difficult to see clearly and make good, or even 'free' choices. Instead, the choices are made from various degrees of 'darkness' or bondage, which are the result of this netted covering. Prayer does not change a person's free will, but it does *release the net*, enabling the person to recognize good and freely choose it. The power of prayer to bring such a release occurs especially when *purity*, as mentioned earlier, has become a greater part of the life of the intercessor.

There are five points I have found to be very helpful in praying for people and their needs. Each point covers a different step in the process of 'releasing this net' and bringing the particular need to God's grace.

A Need for Forgiveness ⒈

The first point is to pray for forgiveness. In this step, we pray for the person, or people, of our intercession to forgive all others and, we include a prayer for all others to forgive this person. We do not have to know where forgiveness is needed, or why. We simply pray that any offences be forgiven; and we pray that any inability to forgive be released and covered in God's mercy. As we bring these individuals and their needs before God, there is a particular need for this prayer of forgiveness. Matthew 6: 14-15 reminds us, *"For if you forgive men their trespasses, your heavenly Father also will forgive you; but if you do not forgive men their trespasses, neither will your Father forgive your trespasses."* And Mark 11:25 is similar: *"And whenever you stand praying, forgive, if you have anything against any one; so that your Father also who is in heaven may forgive you your trespasses."*

Paul mentions another reason in 2 Cor. 2:10-11: *"Any one whom you forgive, I also forgive. What I have forgiven, if I have forgiven anything, has been for your sake in the presence of Christ, to keep Satan from gaining the advantage over us; for we are not ignorant of his designs."*

This prayer, however, also needs to be prayed for the intercessor, because the one who is praying, can likewise be holding on to a resentment or bitterness that could create a hindrance in the intercession. So we say this prayer for ourselves. This prayer of forgiveness is for the purpose of releasing any obstacle that may be creating a block in the flow of God's blessing. To lack forgiveness is a major obstacle, but other obstacles such as fear, worry, resentment, etc., should also be prayed for release. The intercessor should pray for anything that is not from God (hatred, pride, confusion, greed, etc.), to be released and then replaced with those things that are from God (love, humility, peace, and so forth). This first point is a step of removing obstacles.

> *I pray, Lord, for forgiveness for all ways in which I have offended You and other people; and I pray, too, Your forgiveness for those people I intercede for today. I pray, as well, for all those who need to forgive us, and for any inability to forgive that might be held within our hearts. Please give to us Your love so that we can forgive as You forgive, and let there be a release of any obstacles that might hinder the intercessions that are brought to You this day.*

Submitting to God 2

The second point is submission to God. In this step we pray for the person of our intercession to be submitted to God's will, God's authority, and God's love. Since God is perfect in all he does and in all he wills, it is only to our benefit to be in perfect submission to him. We submit all aspects of our intercession, as well. We offer all of this to God's care with complete trust in his loving and divine authority. In this part of intercession we are praying as the words of James 4:7 tell us, *"Submit yourselves therefore to God,"* and Psalm 37:5, *"Commit your way to the Lord; trust in him, and he will act."* This submission is a complete release to God without holding on to anything of, or for, ourselves. It is a confident and steadfast surrender like that written in Lamentations 3: 24-26: *"'The Lord is my portion', says my soul, 'therefore I will hope in him.' The Lord is good to those who wait for him, to the soul that seeks him. It is good that one should wait quietly for the salvation of the Lord."* We pray for those in need to be wholly submitted to God, hoping in him and waiting for his saving grace. This is a step of submission and trust, turning everything over to the Lord.

I pray, Lord, in complete submission to Your perfect and holy will. Help those I pray for to see the good that You so graciously will for our lives, and give them the grace of surrendering all they need to Your care. Please let their own difficulties and suffering not lead them into sin, but let it lead them, instead, to trust in Your Divine Love.

The Blood of Christ 3

The third point is to pray the blood of Christ over the people and their situation. Just as at Passover when the blood of the lamb was put over the doorway to protect the Israelites from the angel of death, we cover the need of our intercession with the blood of Jesus. Scripture speaks of this blood in the Old and the New Testament. Exodus 12:7 refers to the instructions the Lord gave to Moses and Aaron concerning the lamb's blood, so that the plague would pass over their families, *"Then they shall take some of the blood, and put in on the two door posts and the lintel of the houses ... "* In the New Testament, Peter writes of this saving blood as Christ's, *"You know that you were ransomed from the futile ways inherited from your fathers, not with perishable things such as silver or gold, but with the precious blood of Christ, like that of a lamb without blemish or spot."* (1 Pet. 1:18-19) And in his letter to the Ephesians, (2:13) Paul writes, *"But now in Christ Jesus you who once were far off have been brought near in the blood of Christ."* The apostle John also writes of this in his first epistle, *" ... but if we walk in the light, as he is in the light, we have fellowship with one another, and the blood of Jesus his Son cleanses us from all sin."* (1 John. 1:7) Our prayers, in a sense, are simply bringing those in need to this same place of God's grace that is written in scripture: to be *ransomed from futile ways, brought near* to God, and *cleansed from all sin*, by the blood of Christ. We pray this over the people, their families, or any situation in our prayers. This is a step of coming under God's covering.

> *I pray the blood of Christ over those people I intercede for today. I pray, Lord, that through Your precious blood they would be delivered from any harm or evil, any wrong-focus, and any thoughts or actions that might lead them away from You. Cover them, Lord, and allow them the grace of knowing that they are held in Your love.*

Taking on the Mind of Christ

Paul wrote in his first letter to the Corinthians, *"The unspiritual man does not receive the gifts of the Spirit of God, for they are folly to him, and he is not able to understand them because they are spiritually discerned. The spiritual man judges all things, but is himself to be judged by no one. "For who has known the mind of the Lord so as to instruct him?" But we have the mind of Christ."* (1 Cor. 2:14-16) What does it mean to have *the mind of Christ?* We know that when we are going through a difficult time, or experiencing something stressful or fearful, we may be living in that stress or fear, but Christ is not. The Lord is fully aware of our situation since he remains with us and nothing *"in all creation will be able to separate us from the love of God in Christ Jesus our Lord."* (Rom.8:39) But Christ is able to see the same situation we are in and it does not frighten him or cause him to worry. He has, or even more, he is the answer to our problem. Our problems do not make him fearful, and that means they do not have to make us fearful. We can begin to pray for Christ's perspective and his answer to our need. Taking on the mind of Christ means, in one respect, that we begin to see things with the same confident assurance that Christ has in seeing those same things. It does not mean that we see everything with the same clarity and fullness of knowledge that Christ has, but we know the answer is there for us, within God, and that *"in everything God works for good."* (Rom.8:28)

Sometimes in giving spiritual direction I have found it helpful for people to make a list of all the things they are fearful of concerning a particular situation they are in. After the list is finished, I tell them to make another list, along side this one, that describes the perspective they think Christ has about each item on their list. If they are worried about losing a job and every concern that situation would entail, they can begin to view Christ looking at their job situation and try to imagine his response. They can meditate on the peace he has and place themselves in his presence where all peace exists. Even if they do not know exactly what Christ has for them as an answer, they know that he sees the situation and every detail that needs help. It is in this sense that we pray for people to have, or begin to perceive, the mind of Christ. This is a step of giving up our perspective, and therefore our control, to gain the perspective and confident peace of our Lord.

> *I pray now for those people of my intercession to have the mind of Christ. Help them, Lord, to see things from Your pure and holy perspective which contains for us all life, all hope, all truth, and all good. Help those I intercede for to be led in every decision by the grace of Your wisdom. And I pray that others would be able to perceive the mind of Christ and the heart of Christ in those who profess Your name.*

Thanking God for New Life 5

"*The one who sat on the throne said, "Behold, I make all things new." Then he said, "Write these words down, for they are trustworthy and true." (Rev.21:5)* The fifth of these points of intercession is simply the step of praying in agreement with Rev.21:5. We believe that God is receiving our intercessions, and we believe he is answering our need. We pray, then, in gratitude for the new beginning that God is already working to fulfill.

Phil.4:6 reminds us to pray *with thanksgiving*. The thanks we offer to God is an important part of prayer. It is the acknowledgement of God's goodness and faithfulness to provide for his children. So this fifth point is both a step of thanksgiving and a confession of our faith for the good that God desires to do in our lives. We are not professing to know exactly how that good will be manifested, because we have surrendered the need, and therefore the outcome, to the Lord. We know, however, that we can trust in God to do what is best for us, and that the need we have brought before him is being furthered in the process of 'becoming new' in him who makes *"all things new."* When I pray through these points, I use this final one to pray any particular scriptures that seem appropriate to the needs of my prayer, and I include my thanks to God. A simple example of this would be, "Thank you, Lord, that you 'make straight what is crooked' in our lives." (in reference to the scripture we read in Lk.3:5). Or, "Thank you, Lord, that you 'instruct us and teach us in the way we should go.'" (Ps.32:8) A scripture I often close my prayers with is Psalm 145:13, "Thank you, Lord, for being 'faithful in all your words, and gracious in all your deeds.'" Whatever is the particular need of your intercession, a scripture that acknowledges God's faithfulness to provide, puts our attention on the Lord with the gratitude that we should always have in our heart. It is never God who fails us, but we who fail to put our faith in him and acknowledge his goodness.

I thank You, Lord, for the power and the privilege of prayer that allows us into Your presence. Thank You for Your faithfulness in answering the needs that we place in Your care. I am grateful to You for working all these things together for good, and for leading us to new life. I praise You for all You are doing on our behalf. Amen.

In Closing

Prayer is a great gift from God to draw us into deeper union with him - a union in which we actively participate, a union that we freely choose to make with heart, soul, mind, and strength. It is a gift that unites us, as well, with the whole body of Christ, making us one with each other to fulfill Christ's prayer for unity.

How great a gift! How holy and transforming its purpose. How faithfully God uses it to meet our needs and bless us with his presence. These words of Paul can be applied also to prayer: *"Thanks be to God for his inexpressible gift!"* 2 Cor. 9:15

> *"Now to him who is able to accomplish far more than all we ask or imagine, by the power at work within us, to him be glory in the church and in Christ Jesus to all generations, forever and ever. Amen."* Eph.3:20-21

Some of the Questions I have been asked:

Q - When you mention being in God's presence, do you visualize what you see is God the Father, or visualize Jesus, or what?
A - I see in my mind that I am right before Him, as I would be with someone who was right in front of my face. Sometimes I picture the face of Jesus, but most often I just imagine someone's face very close to mine as I would imagine it if I had my eyes closed. I would not be looking at the person then, but could still be aware of their close presence before me. That is the closeness that I am picturing more than an actual face.

Q - If you have been praying for someone's heart to be turned toward God, but you never see any change in the person, even after a long time of interceding, how do you keep from becoming discouraged?
A - You have to continually see the person in God's hands and do not lose heart, or your focus, on God's faithfulness. Sometimes prayer is like planting a small seed in the ground. When we worry or become discouraged, it is because we are looking for the results we want, rather than doing our part which is to pray, leave the need in God's hands, and nurture it with faith and gratitude. We must try to not 'dig up the seed' to see how it is doing. We have to trust in God's timing. Many of the saints were converted after years of faithful prayer for them.

Q - Sometimes I feel as though the Holy Spirit is prompting me to pray a certain way. How do I know if I am praying in the way God wants me to pray, or if it is my own self in the prayers?
A - You may not know, but you can ask God to purify your prayers and the intentions of your heart. I often recognize that the prayers I am saying will suddenly come with a thought that is very unexpected, or I will get a very clear impression of something to add to the prayers. I pray the way I feel I am being led, but also, I have learned to be still before God with an attitude of 'listening' and I wait for

direction before I even begin to pray in a particular way that might be based more on how I see things.

Q - I seem to make progress in my attempts to trust God in my prayers, but then I find myself back in the same thinking patterns of fear and self-absorbed worry. How do I get past this?

A - Make your prayers a continual 'coming to God,' to seek and thank Him. Over time, the focus will be taken off of yourself and grow to be completely on Him. Sometimes we may have to pray the same prayer of surrender over and over and over many times a day, but in that way we are turning to God in our need over and over and over through the day. Eventually we will see his grace begin to change us. Be trusting of God and patient with yourself.

Q - Have you ever felt in prayer that the Lord was asking you to say something to someone, like give them a message? How do you handle that? What if it is something that sounds strange?

A - Yes, I have felt that on several occasions. First, I always ask the Holy Spirit to confirm it some how, and I am almost always surprised at the way the words come back to me again in different, clear, and unexpected ways. Secondly, I make sure that the words I think God may be telling me to say are in likeness to His character, meaning, 'Do these words convey a deep and sincere love for the person? Do they reveal God's mercy and humble compassion? Are they encouraging? In other words, does this 'message' have the Lord's 'signature' on it? Also, I pay close attention if the words come to me with a strong feeling inside, like overwhelming tears or joy or some depth of feeling that I could not suddenly 'make up' inside myself. I might say to the person, "Please correct me if I am wrong, but it keeps coming to me in prayer that .... " Now it is quite possible to have one's own inner focus (on self) get in the way of our ability to 'hear' correctly. So, I pay particular attention to the confirmation of love, peace, humility, compassion, and so forth, being present inside of me. I pay attention also to how I feel about speaking the words, whether I am feeling humble, loving, compassionate, and forgiving, myself, in speaking to them.

Q - Sometimes I feel so small and insignificant before God, it makes me think my prayers are not good enough to bring before Him. That discourages me from praying at times.
A - It is good to realize how 'small' and needy we really are, as long as we continually turn to God in that realization. The Love who created us, though, does not see us as insignificant. As to the prayers, or the way you pray, not seeming to be good enough, that is not for you to decide. Abandon all thoughts that are a self focus and dwell on - and in - God's love, purity, and goodness.

Q - What does it mean to 'pray without ceasing'? And is that really possible?
A - Paul wrote this in his letter to the Thessalonians (1 Thess. 5:17) and it means to be turned to God continuously. We do this in the same way that we might experience a deeply present love for someone, even while we are engaged in other activities, we are keenly aware of the love that is always in our heart and on our minds for the other; or like a mother never forgetting her baby, because her love is so strong she is always inclined toward that child and attentive to its care. And yes, it is possible, because it is what God had in mind for us when we were created.

I pray, Lord, for forgiveness for all ways in which I have offended You and other people, and I pray, too, Your forgiveness for those people I intercede for today. I pray, as well, for all those who need to forgive us, and for any inability to forgive that might be held within our hearts. Please give to us Your love so that we can forgive as You forgive, and let there be a release of any obstacles that might hinder the intercessions that are brought to You this day.

I pray, Lord, in complete submission to Your perfect and holy will. Help those I pray for to see the good that You so graciously will for our lives, and give them the grace of surrendering all they need to Your care. Please let their own difficulties and suffering not lead them into sin, but let it lead them, instead, to trust in Your Divine Love.

I pray the blood of Christ over those people I intercede for today. I pray, Lord, that through Your precious blood they would be delivered from any harm or evil, any wrong-focus, and any thoughts or actions that might lead them away from You. Cover them, Lord, and allow them the grace of knowing that they are held in Your love.

I pray now for those people of my intercession to have the mind of Christ. Help them, Lord, to see things from Your pure and holy perspective which contains for us all life, all hope, all truth, and all good. Help those I intercede for to be led in every decision by the grace of Your wisdom. And I pray that others would be able to perceive the mind of Christ and the heart of Christ in those who profess Your name.

I thank You, Lord, for the power and the privilege of prayer that allows us into Your presence. Thank You for Your faithfulness in answering the needs that we place in Your care. I am grateful to You for working all these things together for good, and for leading us to new life. I praise You for all You are doing on our behalf.
Amen.

[1] The American Heritage Dictionary of the English Language

[2] Strong's Exhaustive Concordance of the Bible, p. 93, Hebrew Dictionary of the O.T., p. 29, 74, Greek Dictionary of the N.T., and Vine's Expository Dictionary of the Old and New Testament Words, p. 267.

[3] Understanding Penance, by Cricket Aull, explains in more detail the benefits of adding a sacrifice to our prayers.

[4] Strong's Exhaustive Concordance of the Bible, p. 38 of Greek Dictionary of the N.T..

[5] Prayers of the Women Mystics, by Ronda De Sola Chervin, Ch. 7, p. 82, taken from The Dialogue, by St. Catherine of Siena, trans. by Suzanne Noffke, O.P. 125.

[6] Omnibus of Sources, p. 707, Major Life of St. Francis by St. Bonaventure, Ch. 10, 3.

[7] Omnibus of Sources, p. 1229. Mirror of Perfection, #95.

[8] Strong's Exhaustive Concordance of the Bible, p. 26, Greek Dictionary of the N.T..

Holy Scriptures are taken from the New American Bible and the Revised Standard Version.

WORKS CITED

The American Heritage Dictionary of the English Language.
Ed. William Morris. Boston, Houghton Mifflin Company, 1976.

Strong's Exhaustive Concordance of the Bible.
James Strong, S.T.D., LL.D., Peabody, Massuchusetts 01961-3473:
Hendrickson Publishers.

Catherine of Siena - The Dialogue. Trans. Suzanne Noffke, O.P.,
New York - Mahwah: Paulist Press, 1980. p. 125.

Omnibus of Sources. Ed. Marion A. Habig, Chicago, Illinois:
Franciscan Herald Press, 1983.

---. "Major Life of St. Francis." St. Bonaventure. Trans. Benen Fahy,
    O.F.M. p. 707.
---. "Mirror of Perfection." Trans. Leo Sherley-Price, p. 1229.